JOY

JOY

Choosing Hope in an Age of Uncertainty

JEREN ROWELL

f

THE FOUNDRY
PUBLISHING®

Copyright © 2022 by Jeren Rowell

The Foundry Publishing®
PO Box 419527
Kansas City, MO 64141
thefoundrypublishing.com

ISBN 978-0-8341-4120-9

Cover design: J.R. Caines
Interior design: Sharon Page

The internet addresses, email addresses, and phone numbers in this book are accurate at the time of publication. They are provided as a resource. The Foundry Publishing® does not endorse them or vouch for their content or permanence.

To Stephen—
the most genuinely joyful person I know

"Restore to me the joy of your salvation."

—*Psalm 51:12*

Contents

Introduction

MANY YEARS AGO, during a weeklong personal retreat, I read a book by Canadian author Mike Mason
that captured my spiritual imagination. It was *Champagne for the Soul: Celebrating God's Gift of Joy.* In
that book, Mike reports on a ninety-day spiritual journey in which he deepened his understanding of joy.
Throughout my Christian life, I never thought very
deeply about the grace of Christian joy. Mike's conviction is that "you can take hold of joy as simply as
turning on a light switch in a dark room."[1] He is not
discounting the grace of God but simply recognizing
the "response-ability" we are given to choose joy. The
story of Mike's pilgrimage confronted and challenged
me. I began to face the truth in a new way—that is,
while my life in Christ could be characterized by words
such as "devotion," "commitment," and even "sacri-
fice," the word "joy" was not really part of my expe-
riential vocabulary. By the Spirit's guidance through
Mike's words, I came to a new place in my spiritual
journey about joy. It so enlivened my heart that as a
pastor I couldn't wait to share with my congregation
what I had learned.

The chapters that follow are the result of six sermons that were preached to the people of the Shaw-
nee, Kansas, Church of the Nazarene during the Easter
season of 2004. The post-9/11 anxiety we were experiencing in those days is part of what led me to address

the need for a recovery of the grace of Christian joy. It was clear that as a people, the stress, worry, and fear we were experiencing did not reflect the hope-filled gospel of Jesus Christ. Enabled by God's grace, these sermons sparked congregational conversation, prayer, and healing. This experience has compelled me to offer the content of these sermons here.

It seems obvious that our collective anxiety as Christians in the early twenty-first century has only increased. I am writing now as we are just emerging from the 2020 COVID pandemic and while we are still in the midst of the political, racial, and social unrest that seems to find its way to the forefront of our daily conversations. The church has not fared well, too often reflecting the shrill sounds of an anxious and angry world more than the life-giving sounds of the peaceable kingdom of Christ Jesus. The cultural distance, rancor, and divisiveness of recent years have harmed the witness of the church at a time when we who recognize the reign of God in Christ Jesus should be leading with faith, hope, and love. These reflections are offered in the hope that we might be encouraged today, as I and my people were encouraged in those days when we sought the graced renewal of Christian joy.

My deep thanks to Mike Mason for sparking this journey. I recommend the reading of his book. And thanks to the good people of my beloved congregation during those days. Your responsiveness to your pastor's preaching was an occasion of great joy in my life.

—Jeren Rowell
Nazarene Theological Seminary
Pentecost 2021

1

The Ten Commandments of Joy

*Shout for joy to the L*ORD*, all the earth.*
   *Worship the L*ORD *with gladness;*
   come before him with joyful songs.
*Know that the L*ORD *is God.*
   It is he who made us, and we are his;
   we are his people, the sheep of his pasture.
Enter his gates with thanksgiving
   and his courts with praise;
   give thanks to him and praise his name.
*For the L*ORD *is good and his love endures forever;*
   his faithfulness continues through all generations.
                                        —Psalm 100

"JOY" is a prominent word in the Bible. If we want to know more joy in our lives, there is good news: the Bible has much to say about the gift of joy. A simple concordance check reveals that the word "joy" and its synonyms used to translate the pertinent biblical words appear some four hundred times in the Scriptures.

Much has been made in the past of the claim that happiness is different from joy. The idea is that happiness is based on "happenings" or circumstances, but joy is a spiritual gift from God. This distinction can be helpful, because God's people have discovered the mystery of experiencing true joy even when the circumstances of life are not particularly happy. However, when applied to the biblical texts, the distinction between happiness and joy is perhaps not so sharp. What does become clear, however, is the truth about where the source of true happiness or joy is located. You may immediately have an idea about that source, but don't go there too quickly. The answer may surprise you.

Why a book about joy? One of my disciplines as a pastor was to go on a personal retreat every year to plan my preaching for the following year. Several key questions guided me, and among them was the question of what the people in my congregation seemed to be dealing with in their daily lives. Through conversation and prayer, I came to sense the "cries and needs" of my people, which then became part of a plan for biblical preaching. In other words, I asked, What does the Bible have to say about this or that concern of the people I love and for whom I have spiritual responsibility?

One year during that annual retreat, I was struck by the realization that for all the joyful talk that is part of our faith, real happiness often seems elusive. There is a perfectly sensible reason for this. Life in this world can be serious and often just plain difficult. You can see it on the faces of people everywhere. I notice it in the aisles of the grocery store, in the doctor's waiting room, when glancing at the faces of the other drivers at a four-way stop, and even on the faces of the people with whom I worship every Sunday. We are stressed, distracted, worried, and tired.

To be candid, it's more than what I have noticed; it is also where I've walked personally. The very year that brought this pastoral emphasis on joy also contained one of the darkest seasons of my spiritual journey. There were many seeds of that "dark night of the soul," but one Wednesday morning in November my emotional well-being came crashing down in a pitiful heap of utter helplessness. I literally could not get out of bed. Through the "care-full" ministry of my wife, sisters, and physician, I not only recovered but also learned some deep lessons about walking by faith.

Perhaps you find yourself just now at a place where your life is full of joy and even happiness. If this is your experience, praise God and know that this gift carries with it a responsibility to help others who are struggling. Or perhaps you can relate to the words of the prophet Joel when he cried, "The vine is dried up and the fig tree is withered; . . . all the trees of the field . . . are dried up. Surely the people's joy is withered away" (Joel 1:12). Sometimes our journey takes us into a strange land where nothing looks familiar, and we feel adrift in a sea of threatening emotions. When this happens, we need healing, and this often takes time. We also have the opportunity to go deeper into the knowledge and experience of genuine joy. And for this journey, the Scriptures can guide us.

There are several different types of psalms, and it is important to know which type we are dealing with so that we can hear it as it was intended to be heard by the community of Israel. As the heading in your translation probably indicates, Psalm 100 is a psalm of thanksgiving. It may have been written to accompany the thank-offering ritual in the temple. It was certainly a song used by worshippers as they entered the presence of the Lord, the way we often hear it today. The language is lofty and uplifting, no doubt, but there is more going on here than lifting our spirits. This worship hymn is full of imperatives or commands. Nearly every line presses an imperative into the worship of God's people as they proceed through the gates of the temple into the inner areas where the very presence of the Lord was understood to reside. Therefore, the psalm can be understood under the heading "The Ten Commandments of Joy." This is because these imperatival phrases, these admonitions, are trying to teach us something important about how real happiness is experienced.

Here are the "Ten Commandments of Joy" in Psalm 100 (emphasis added):

1. "*Shout* for joy to the LORD" (v. 1).

2. "*Worship* the LORD with gladness" (v. 2).

3. *"Come* before him with joyful songs" (v. 2).

4. *"Know* that the LORD is God" (v. 3).

5. *Know* that "it is he who made us" (v. 3).

6. *Know* that "we are his people" (v. 3).

7. *"Enter* his gates with thanksgiving" (v. 4).

8. *Enter* "his courts with praise" (v. 4).

9. *"Give* thanks to him" (v. 4).

10. *"Praise* his name" (v. 4).

I will not examine each of these separately as if studying the Decalogue (the Ten Commandments of Exodus 20); instead, I want to draw attention to the way these phrases are oriented to God. These commands are not static rules but gracious invitations to move in close to the heart of God and there to experience real life, yes, real happiness! The foundation of joy is described for us in the final verse: "For the LORD is good. His unfailing love continues forever, and his faithfulness continues to each generation" (v. 5, NLT). The abundant life to which God calls us and for which God has given us grace is not rooted in what we can do to make everything in our lives nice and happy. The joy that the Bible promises is rooted in the character of God.

Do you remember the story of Martin and Gracia Burnham? They were the missionaries from Wichita, Kansas, who were kidnapped in May of 2001 in the Philippines. Before the Philippine military launched a

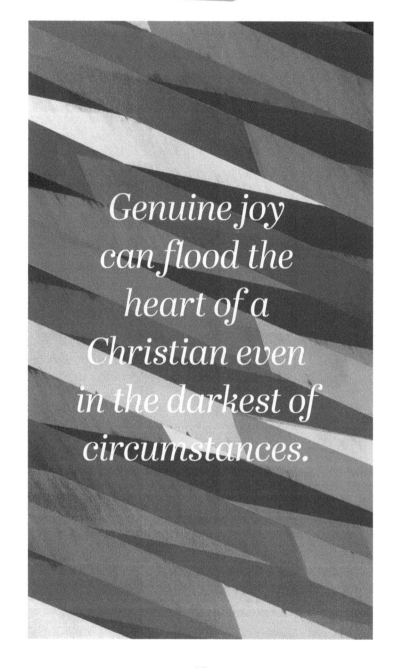

Genuine joy can flood the heart of a Christian even in the darkest of circumstances.

surprise attack on the kidnappers, which resulted in the death of Martin and the rescue of Gracia, the husband and wife shared their thoughts with each other. Martin's brother Doug said at Martin's memorial service, "Martin and Gracia had really been thinking that there would be a chance they would not make it out alive. . . . Martin said to Gracia, 'The Bible says to serve the Lord with gladness. Let's go out all the way. Let's serve him all the way with gladness.'" After praying, reciting Scripture, and singing, they settled down to rest. Soon the military rescue began, with its accompanying gunfire.[2]

They were following what Paul and Silas had modeled from the very beginning of the Christian movement (Acts 16:25). Genuine joy can flood the heart of a Christian even in the darkest of circumstances. But experiencing this is no accident. We seem to think of joy as something that happens *to* you, kind of a whimsical thing. We almost put "joyful" and "lucky" into the same category. The psalmist places joy on a plane entirely different from happenstance. The call of Psalm 100 is to embrace a particular mindset. We see this in the imperative of verse 3: "*Know* that the Lord is God"—that is, acknowledge, know, think this way. "Consider it pure joy, my brothers and sisters," the Lord's brother would say, "whenever you face trials of many kinds" (James 1:2). In other words, this is a *choice*. Joy is a *decision* that we make. It is a grace-enabled decision for sure, but our response to the truth of God's presence and provision is called forth by the power of the Holy Spirit, and we are invited to *choose* joy.

That's why joy, as the psalmist is talking about it, is a commandment. It may seem strange to you to think about joy as a commandment. In the experience of our daily lives, joy can seem as elusive as a dream. The witness of the Scriptures, however, is that joy is a present and available gift to us by a loving heavenly Father. Jesus placed joy as the fruit of obedience. He said, "I have told you these things so that you will be filled with my joy. Yes, your joy will overflow!" (John 15:11, NLT).

Can God really command us to be happy? Jesus commanded us to "love one another" (v. 12, KJV), and we don't seem to chafe at that command. So why would we argue with the command to rejoice? Mike Mason helps with this explanation:

> In the case of love, we know that we ought to do it, and we also know that we can. If we don't love, it's not because we cannot but because we will not. . . .
>
> It's the same with joy. Happiness is a choice. As Abraham Lincoln put it, *"People are just about as happy as they make up their mind to be."* What we lack as Christians isn't just the will to believe

the gospel, but the will to be happy about what we believe. Indeed our lack of joy is a sign of unbelief.[3]

This reminds me of a much older but equally powerful challenge given by Oswald Chambers in his book *Studies in the Sermon on the Mount.* Chambers is arguing that discernment in spiritual matters is not obtained by intellect but by obedience. "If things are dark to us spiritually, it is because there is something we will not do. Intellectual darkness comes because of ignorance; spiritual darkness comes because of something I do not intend to obey."[4]

I know that sometimes our faculties of mind and will can be "dis-eased." To tell someone with depression or mental illness to "just choose joy" is indeed a cruel and simplistic response. However, there is still a decision that a depressed person can make here. It's the decision to accept help from others. A person should accept the necessary medical and psychological help so that he or she can begin moving through the depression to a healthy mental capacity.

There are two dimensions of joy. First, it is part of the fruit of the Spirit, which is the possession of everyone who has received Christ Jesus as Savior, no exceptions. But second, it entails a profound spiritual discipline. There is something about exercising the will—about intentionally choosing joy—that strengthens the ability to experience joy more often and more thoroughly. Joy is a gift of grace, no doubt, but part of that gift involves a call to *do* something. This call is observed in the commands we hear in Psalm 100—commands to worship, sing songs of praise, give thanks to God, and so on. Joy does not rest on a foundation of feelings or emotions but on a foundation of worship and spiritual discipline.

Perhaps some of us struggle to experience joy because we are so disengaged from worship. There is a close connection here. The word "worship" has fallen on hard times. When many people today speak of "worship," they mean a service or music or some particular activity. Worship really means "to serve." To worship is to serve the purposes and glory of God. It means to acknowledge in our lives the exclusive rule and reign of God. Joy can only be known when our lives are rightly oriented to God as the source of everything. Many Christians do not have joy because their loyalties are compromised, scattered, and divided. The great Bible scholar Walter Brueggemann says that to practice the admonitions of Psalm 100 in the context of a world like ours is "an act of sanity, whereby we may be re-clothed in our rightful minds."[5]

In 1967, a diving accident left then seventeen-year-old Joni Eareckson a quadriplegic. She has become well known for her courageous and effective life in the face of such debilitating circumstances.

Some years ago, Joni was speaking at a women's conference, and during a break, one of the participants approached her with a question. She asked Joni how she was able to be so joyful. Joni admitted that she was not the source of her joy. She then recounted a typical morning of living with her disability. She described her dependence on a friend to help her bathe, dress, brush her teeth, and send her on her way. Joni then said that before beginning this daily routine, she would ask God to give her his smile for the day, because she did not have one of her own. So when her friend would come to help her, Joni would "give her a smile sent straight from heaven." Joni then added, "And so . . . whatever joy you see today was hard won this morning."[6]

Think about that for your life. What would it mean to experience a "joy hard won"? It may mean coming into a whole new understanding of what it means to worship God. Do you know that worship is far more than what happens in the sanctuary on a Sunday morning? Worship is about the orientation of your whole life to the holy love and will of God. It may mean that you need to work at changing your mind, which is possible by the transforming grace of God (Rom. 12:1-2). You may need to change how you are thinking about yourself and about your place in the world or among God's people. Maybe you need new thoughts about God and what God thinks of you. Are you confident God absolutely delights in you? Don't dismiss that idea. God absolutely does take delight in you! There are plenty of Bible texts that speak about this glad reality. Psalm 147:11 says, "The LORD delights in those who fear him, who put their hope in his unfailing love."

The way to experience real happiness is to align your mind, your will, your spirit, and even your body with the truth of who God is and with the truth of who you are in God's sight. "Know that the LORD is God. It is he who made us, and we are his; we are his people, the sheep of his pasture" (Ps. 100:3).

Therefore, beloved of God, "Worship the Lord with joy!"

For Reflection

- How do contemporary ideas of joy agree or disagree with what the Bible seems to be saying?

- If joy is a gift, then what part does our will play in experiencing joy?

- How does the connection between joy and suffering in this chapter strike you? Have you witnessed someone exhibit joy during suffering?

Closing Prayer

Lord of all power and might, the author and giver of all good things: Graft in our hearts the love of your Name; increase in us true religion; nourish us with all goodness; and bring forth in us the fruit of good works; through Jesus Christ our Lord, who lives and reigns with you and the Holy Spirit, one God, for ever and ever. Amen.[7]

2

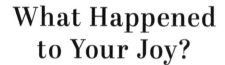

What Happened to Your Joy?

So now that you know God (or should I say, now that God knows you), why do you want to go back again and become slaves once more to the weak and useless spiritual principles of this world? . . . Where is that joyful and grateful spirit you felt then?

—Galatians 4:9, 15, NLT

WE SAW IN CHAPTER 1 that the Bible frames joy as a gift of God's grace, but it also involves decisions we make. Our decisions have a consequential effect on joy. That effect has to do with whether our lives are oriented to God and aligned with the truth of who God is and who we are in God's sight.

The practical problem is that for all the joyful talk that is part of our religion, real happiness often seems to be as elusive as a butterfly. I was struck by the words of psychologist Kim Hall, who, in an interview several years ago, was reflecting on how people today want immediate happiness, believing they have an inalienable right to it. That's not a surprise, but then Dr. Hall said, "People walk into my office and say they are Christians, but I see no difference except that they want to be happy and expect God to make it so."[8]

What has happened to our happiness? Why is it that study after study is revealing little difference in life choices, satisfaction, and emotional health between professed Christians and those who make no profession of faith? Could it be that even Christians have lost sight of the true ground of joy? Could it be that despite what we profess, we are actually searching in the same places the world searches and that doing so is leaving us just as flat?

It's that very concern that is driving this passionate plea from Paul to the Galatian Christians. These Christians forgot their true identity, and consequently, Paul noticed that they were no longer the free and joyful people they once were. I think I understand the heart of Paul here. As a pastor, I often looked over my congregation and wondered, *What happened to our happiness?* I could see the choices we were making. I could hear the stress and tension in our voices. I saw the anxiety on our faces. Some of this is a natural part of life in this fallen world. However, I think we must be willing to tell the truth about ourselves. Too often, even as Christians, we look in the wrong places for happiness.

I'm not pointing a judgmental finger. This is not only what I've observed but also where I've walked. Part of my own journey in honestly staring down my joylessness was to face some truths about myself that were hard to face. I can relate to Paul's cry in this passage: "Where is that joyful and grateful spirit you felt then?" (Gal. 4:15, NLT). As I investigated what is behind that cry, I think there is much we can learn from the situation of these early Christians that applies to us.

The clear implication of Paul's question to the Galatians is that Christians should be living a life of joy and that if we are not, something has gone wrong. If we are not joyful, we need to ask some hard questions about what has sabotaged our joy. For most of us, coming to know Jesus as our Savior almost always seems to begin with great joy. Nothing is sweeter than being present when someone comes to faith in Christ for the first time. I hope you've had that joy-filled experience. One of the delights of being around new Christians is sensing their joy and happiness at what Jesus has done and is doing for them. Joy is a natural part of what it means to be a Christian. If we've lost sight of joy, regaining it may be partly a matter of remembering.

Throughout the story of God narrated for us in the Bible, the people of God are often admonished to remember. This memory is not simply a recounting of history but also the memory of how God acted, provided, protected, and guided the people through peril and blessing. It's like marriage, which begins with a joyful celebration. Wedding days are among the happiest days we experience, yet too often the joyfulness of those days slides into dull routines and predictable patterns.

Many of us can reflect on the early days of our new faith in Christ as a season when the whole world seemed new. Colors were brighter, music was richer, relationships deepened, and even some of our struggles were overcome with ease. And why not? When we are united with Christ by faith, we are new creation people. The risen Jesus said, "Look, I am making everything new!" (Rev. 21:5, NLT). This is true for all of God's good creation, and it is the project of God's redeeming and reconciling of the world to God (2 Cor. 5:18-19). Yet this new creation work is also intensely personal. Do you remember the glorious joy with which you first welcomed Jesus into your life? Why would you now settle for less? What is cutting you off from that joy in the present? That's the question that Paul puts to these Galatian congregations.

There is a clear answer. Paul says to them earlier in this letter, "You foolish Galatians! Who has bewitched you? . . . You were running a good race. Who cut in on you to keep you from obeying the truth?" (Gal. 3:1; 5:7). We get a clue to what happened in the opening chapter. There Paul says to them, "I am astonished that you are so quickly deserting the one who called you to live in the grace of Christ and are turning to a different gospel" (1:6). Here's what was happening. Paul had come to them during his missionary work and preached that salvation is by faith in Jesus Christ and not by any other way that people sometimes attempt to earn God's favor. The Galatians received that good news, and they experienced freedom in Christ. But after Paul left, something else began to happen. A

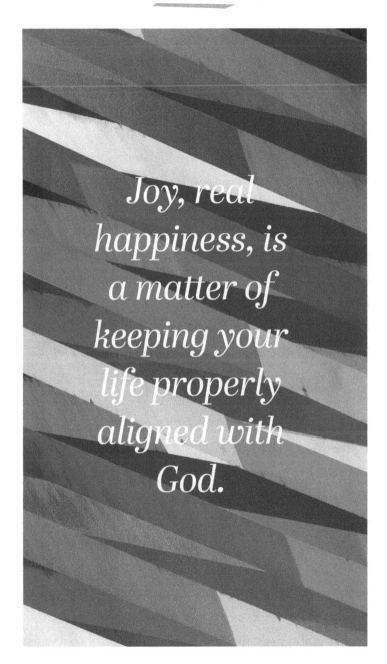

Joy, real happiness, is a matter of keeping your life properly aligned with God.

group of folks known as Judaizers arrived and began to teach the Galatians that the only way to be a true Christian is to also take upon oneself all the burden of the law. To be accepted as God's children, believers had to be circumcised and observe the traditions and rules of Judaism. Some of the Galatians began to believe this teaching.

This misguided approach to salvation had prompted a major controversy early in the Christian movement. Even the great apostle Peter sometimes struggled to keep clear that salvation is by grace through faith. In fact, in Galatians 2, Paul reports that he and Peter had an actual confrontation over this issue. On the one hand, Peter would preach to the Gentiles that salvation was for all, but on the other hand, when he was around the Judaizers, he would sometimes force the Gentiles to follow the Jewish customs. This issue comes to a head in Acts 15, but not before a lot of new Christians received some very confusing teachings.

In the meantime, many Galatians lost their focus on the freedom and joy they once had in Christ, and they returned to the burden of the law. Paul says to them in Galatians 3, "Are you so foolish? After beginning by means of the Spirit, are you now trying to finish by means of the flesh?" (v. 3). This is what happened to their happiness. They didn't totally turn their backs on Christ, but they began to focus on wrong priorities, and that began to sabotage their joy.

I am suggesting that this very thing can happen to us. What robs us of joy and steals our happiness is not so much the failure of life's circumstances to go the way we would like. The real culprit is that without even realizing it, we begin to serve other gods. Some of us begin to believe that our salvation is not only in the gospel of grace but also in working hard to be good or in exhibiting the behavior others insist makes for a good Christian. This may explain why some professing Christians can be some of the most uptight and joyless people that we know. This ought not to be.

Others of us have sabotaged our happiness because we began to believe the messages that our culture sends us every day. We say we know what is real and true, but the choices we make betray something else. We work ourselves to death trying to pay off the debts of a hundred things that we thought would provide us some happiness. Or we become angry and bitter because life just hasn't treated us right or because people disappointed us. Perhaps our career isn't what we thought it would be, our spouse let us down, or the church hasn't noticed and appreciated us. There are a hundred ways to describe it, but the essence is the same. We get our eyes off Jesus, who is the only real source of our happiness, and we set our eyes on people or things that can never measure up to the hunger of our hearts.

God created us to know and experience delight. It's part of who we are. The desire for happiness is not a bad desire, but we begin looking for it in the wrong places. Thomas Aquinas said, "No one can live without delight and that is why a man deprived of spiritual joy goes over to carnal pleasures."[9] If you find yourself constantly getting dragged back into behaviors and thoughts that you despise and really don't want in your life, it's partly because your heart hungers for delight. However, in a vacuum of true God-given joy, this world entices you to believe that delight can be found through what the Bible calls "the lust of the flesh, and the lust of the eyes, and the pride of life" (1 John 2:16, KJV).

May I ask you a difficult question? I've asked it of myself, so I know that it's not an easy one to face. Nevertheless, we must face it honestly if we're going to have any hope of recovering the first love and joy that God wanted for us when, through his Son, he saved us from trying to save ourselves. Here's the question: What compromised choices or unhealthy patterns are sabotaging your joy? If you can relate to the question "What happened to my happiness?" then there is likely an identifiable reason why joy eludes you. It may be about whom you believe God to be or about whom you believe yourself to be. Perhaps it's about what you deserve or think you deserve. It may be about choices you are making that will never lead you to a place of rest in God's provision. It may be a spirit of rebellion or disobedience deep down that may even be hidden from all those around you, except God. It may be about that secret sin that is eating away at your soul.

"What happened to all your joy?" (see Gal. 4:15, NLT). "You were running a good race. Who cut in on you?" (5:7). Could you, by God's grace, face the answer to that question honestly? Remember what Paul says to the Galatians in chapter 5: "It is for freedom that Christ has set us free. Stand firm, then, and do not let yourselves be burdened again by a yoke of slavery" (v. 1). Joy is not a matter of luck. Joy is not something that just happens to you if you're lucky enough to have things work out right. Joy, real happiness, is a matter of keeping your life properly aligned with God and of refusing to dwell in the lifeless lies of the world. Joy is not an elusive dream. Joy is the gift of God to you right now. The way to experience real happiness and joy is to repent from the thoughts, choices, and beliefs that move you away from trusting totally in God as the source of your life.

Galatians 4:11 captures my attention. Paul says, "I am afraid for you" (NKJV). Let that sink in for a moment. I think I can relate to what Paul is expressing here. I am afraid for us as God's people. I see how we gather in communities of faith week after week and hear the truth of what God has provided, yet so often we fail to take hold of it as our inheritance and blessing. Take hold, loved ones! By the grace of God, joy is yours to receive. Remember who you are—the beloved of God, a people of his own redeeming. Rejoice!

For Reflection

- What are some of the temptations for seeking joy that this world offers?

- How can we discern the difference between authentic joy and temporal happiness?

- When facing suffering, what are some things we should remember or should do to recognize God's gift of joy? What is the role of the community of faith in such circumstances?

Closing Prayer

Grant us, Lord, not to be anxious about earthly things, but to love things heavenly; and even now, while we are placed among things that are passing away, to hold fast to those that shall endure; through Jesus Christ our Lord, who lives and reigns with you and the Holy Spirit, one God, for ever and ever. Amen.[10]

3

24/7 Joy

Rejoice in the Lord always. I will say it again: Rejoice!
—Philippians 4:4

DOES IT EVER seem to you that some of the Bible's claims are just impossibly overoptimistic? The Bible makes some grand and glorious claims for our lives. But let's be candid: Don't they sometimes seem a bit unrealistic?

Now don't get me wrong—I don't doubt that the Bible is true. We understand the Holy Book to be our final rule of faith and practice. We take the Bible very seriously. We believe that the written Word becomes a living Word by the power of the Holy Spirit speaking to us. I am sure most of us truly believe this, but then the Bible says such things as, "You are dead to sin" (see Rom. 6:11). It says, "You have the mind of Christ" (see 1 Cor. 2:16). It says, "Pray without ceasing" (1 Thess. 5:17, KJV). Really? It says, "Rejoice in the Lord *always*" (Phil. 4:4, emphasis added). Does that throw you off a little? "Rejoice in the Lord *always.*"

I mentioned in chapter 1 that people often want to make a distinction between the words "joy" and "happiness." The problem is that the Bible doesn't usually make that distinction. The words themselves are distinct, but in meaning and application, they are fairly interchangeable. However, I think I know why we want to make the distinction. Maybe we want to place "joy" entirely in the supernatural realm because we don't experience it much in the natural realm. Oh, we have some happiness, maybe even quite a bit of happiness, but "rejoice in the Lord *always*"? Is that realistic? We know that many are the days when joy seems far away and elusive. And yet the Scriptures keep insisting that joy is the possession of every child of God. It's put in terms, not of "will be," but of "here and now."

The fruit of the Spirit is an integrated package of character qualities that every person who has received Jesus has received into his or her life. That package is outlined in Galatians 5. You probably know this: "The fruit of the Spirit is love, . . ." (v. 22). What's next? Right! It's "joy." It's a package deal. Joy comes with being a Christian. No extra charge. It is essential, and it is basic to what it means to be a follower of the Lord Jesus Christ. If you are a Christian, you have joy. Perhaps for some of us it just hasn't yet worked its way from the inside to the outside.

The text from Philippians sounds happy, but it may also be bothersome: "Rejoice in the Lord always" (4:4). What exactly is meant by "always," and how does that work? Clearly there are times in life of sadness, grief, stress, disappointment, and pain. Where is this "always joy" in those times? Is the apostle Paul really suggesting that there is for us an experience of "24/7 joy"? It sure does sound like it. But if it's true, then I think we have some work to do to understand how this really functions in a Christian's life.

After Paul says "Rejoice in the Lord always," he goes on: "I will say it again: Rejoice" (v. 4). Why did he say it again? Well, remember that when this letter to the Philippian church was first heard, it was read aloud to the church. They didn't have printed copies of it, as we do, so when Paul sent the letter, someone had to get up and read it to the congregation. I can imagine what happened when the reader came toward the end. Maybe Paul knew what would happen too. "Rejoice in the Lord always." Suddenly people we're poking each other and saying, "What did he say? Did I hear that right?" So Paul adds in the letter, "I will say it again." In other words, "Yes, folks you heard me right. Rejoice always."

I think Paul was aware of the mental block people might have over this verse. In fact, these verses come right after Paul writes about some serious conflicts in the church. One issue he addresses concerns the tension between two women (vv. 2-3). In this case, Paul names the women and entreats them to reconcile. (Can you imagine being one of those two women the day this letter was read?) The other conflict was over people entering the church and trying to convince these new Christians that grace wasn't enough (3:1-14). Paul really lets them have it. He calls them "dogs" and "mutilators of the flesh" (v. 1). Yes, I think Paul was aware of the challenge of "rejoice always."

By the way, do you know where Paul was when he was composing this letter for the Philippian church? He was in jail. He was in chains. "Rejoice in the Lord always" (4:4). Maybe we'd better listen closely. Maybe our brother Paul discovered something about how to experience real happiness. Maybe he really did know that 24/7 joy is possible.

The moment we hear this, we get stuck on that little word "always," and our hearts sink. And so, we overlook the key phrase in this entire text. Do you see it? Three little words: "in the Lord." Those are critical words. Nowhere does the Bible exhort us to do anything in our own strength. The whole Christian life is "in the Lord," right? So, what specifically does Paul tell us in this passage about how to know the reality of 24/7 joy? Remember that joy is not simply a feeling but a way of thinking. It's a decision that we make to orient our lives to God and not to the world. We sabotage our joy when we arrange our lives around the values and priorities of this world instead of the kingdom of God. To be more specific, let me mention three key things that we can draw from this passage about how to experience this "always joy," this 24/7 joy, that Paul preaches.

First, nothing will kill your joy faster than a broken relationship. It's no accident that in the first verses of Philippians 4, Paul entreats these two Christian sisters to repair their relationship. We don't really know what the issue was, but it doesn't really matter. The truth is that any strained relationship in the body of Christ will keep you from the full experience of God's joy. Could it be that to experience the fullness of God's 24/7 joy, you need to repair a broken relationship with someone? It is not about who was right and who was wrong or about winning or losing. It is about surrendering to the lordship of Jesus in all things.

Second, releasing anxiety is the key to experiencing Christian joy. Easier said than done, you say? Perhaps, but Paul tells us exactly how to do it. I can testify that the guidance Paul gives here about releasing anxiety, when taken seriously and practiced faithfully, really does work! Look again at verse 6: "Do not be anxious about anything, but in every situation, by prayer and petition, . . ." How often do we carry around our worries and run them over and over again in our minds rather than truly talking to the Lord about them? You know what happens when we do that, don't you? They feel bigger than they really are.

Verse 6 continues: "with thanksgiving, . . ." What do we give thanks for? We give thanks when we remember the blessings that have come, the ways that

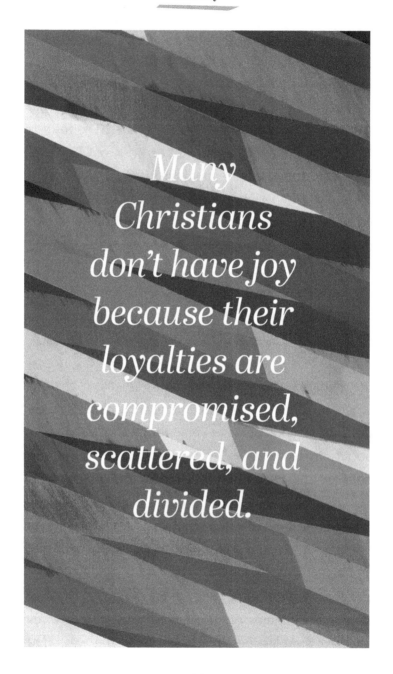

Many Christians don't have joy because their loyalties are compromised, scattered, and divided.

God has been faithful in the past. So "with thanksgiving" means, "Remember how God has helped you before—God's going to do it again."

Verse 6 concludes: "present your requests to God." This is not approaching God as if God were a great cosmic vending machine where we make our requests and then automatically get the desired results. Instead, this is like talking to a friend. It means going to our Father and pouring out our hearts to him, and as we do, something wonderful begins to happen: "And the peace of God, which transcends all understanding, will guard your hearts and your minds in Christ Jesus" (v. 7). I know that this works. I know that this is true! I have experienced it again and again. It goes back to the decision to think and live in what is true and not in what could be, might be, or should have been.

The third thing has to do with the power of the mind. Notice that verses 8 and 9 are discussing what we've already observed. Christian joy does not rest on a foundation of emotions or feelings but on a foundation of a life rightly oriented to God. So much of this has to do with how we *think*. It has to do with whether or not our thoughts are aligned with God's thoughts— that is, the truth about who God is, who we are, and what matters most in life. Many Christians don't have joy because their loyalties are compromised, scattered, and divided.

What is it that God is really offering here? If we live in the truth of these verses, does that mean we are going to feel happy 168 hours a week? Probably not. Does it mean we will never be sad or never experience grief and sorrow in our lives? Of course not. The "always joy" Paul mentions here is intricately connected to the "peace" that "transcends all understanding" (v. 7). And what does this "peace" stand guard over? Our hearts and minds (v. 7). When we talk about joy, we're not talking about a feeling of hilariousness. We're talking about a deep-settled peace that our lives are in God's hands and that no matter what happens, we are safe and secure.

Bethany Hamilton, once ranked as the best amateur teen surfer in Hawaii, lost her arm to a tiger shark. You may remember the story. I can't imagine what it must be like for a fifteen-year-old athlete to face living the rest of her life without an arm. Do you know what Bethany began doing after her devastating injury? Here are just a few examples. After her initial recovery, she began raising money to help a man regain his eyesight. While in New York City for a news interview, she gave a homeless person her ski coat. She's been consistently doing that kind of thing. Her pastor, as quoted by *USA Today*, said, "She's looking forward to the future. She's asking herself, 'How can I show the world I still have a life, that I enjoy my life, and that my life is filled with joy?'"[11]

As a pastor, I've learned that our expectations of God are sometimes so inverted that when life turns sour, many of us don't run to God for refuge; instead, we blame God for the way things are. We can't blame God and rejoice in the Lord at the same time. What makes the difference is not any feeling, any circumstance, or anything we can produce. It is releasing everything into God's hands.

What do you need to release into God's hands? What is sabotaging your joy? Is it a broken relationship? Is it a false expectation of God? Is it a sense of profound disappointment in the way your life has turned out? You need to find out what it is and then let it go. That's the only way you will be free enough to receive what God has designed for you. I like the way my friend Jim McIntosh says it: "Jesus can give you a joy that the devil can't put the brakes on!" That is "always joy"—24/7 joy.

Is that overly optimistic? Well, perhaps it depends on who creates that joy. If it's up to us, then it is overly optimistic, but if it is a gift of God, well—is there enough power in the cross and resurrection of Jesus to bring 24/7 joy to your life? There is indeed! Thanks be to God!

For Reflection

- Why do you think the idea of "rejoice always" is hard for us to imagine in real life? What are some possible misconceptions about Christian joy?

- Have you ever witnessed authentic joy in the life of someone who was going through difficulties? What could that person's life teach you about knowing joy in any circumstance?

- This chapter lists three key things that Christians may need to address to experience 24/7 joy. Which of them speaks to you about your own Christian growth?

Closing Prayer

Almighty and merciful God, it is only by your gift that your faithful people offer you true and laudable service: Grant that we may run without stumbling to obtain your heavenly promises; through Jesus Christ our Lord, who lives and reigns with you and the Holy Spirit, one God, now and for ever. Amen.[12]

4

Joy in the Desert

Though the fig tree does not bud
and there are no grapes on the vines,
though the olive crop fails
and the fields produce no food,
though there are no sheep in the pen
and no cattle in the stalls,
yet I will rejoice in the LORD,
I will be joyful in God my Savior.
—Habakkuk 3:17-18

DURING THE TIME I was preaching this series of messages in my church, I went to the hospital to pray with someone who was facing a major surgery. I walked into the pre-op area where the nurses and doctors were getting everything ready. As I rounded the corner, the patient looked in my direction and said wistfully, "Pastor, I'm *trying* to be happy!"

One reason pastors enjoy preaching a sermon series has to do with the "congregational conversation" that occurs during the upcoming weeks. I enjoyed the dialogue in my congregation during the weeks I preached these messages. It became obvious that a renewal of joy was a deep need in all our lives. I intuitively knew this as a pastor. I could clearly see that in our life together, genuine joy had fallen on hard times. I was noticing stress and frustration, tiredness and disappointment, much more than I was noticing joy and

51

happiness. I also confessed to my people that it was my own experience as well as my observation.

About halfway through the series, I realized that something new was happening. It was not only happening in my people but also in me. It dawned on me that God really was renewing my joy! I was thinking differently than I had been a few weeks earlier. As a result of this new thinking, this "renewing of [the] mind," as Paul puts it in Romans 12:2, I was also feeling different. My heart was lighter, and my hope was keener.

Three key truths were beginning to take root in the congregation:

1. *Joy is a gift of God.* It is part of the fruit of the Spirit, which is the possession of everyone who has received Jesus as the forgiver and leader of his or her life.

2. *Happiness is a choice.* Joy is not first a feeling but a decision that we make to open the gift and receive not only *what* God wants to give but also the *way* in which God wants to give it.

3. *Our choices often sabotage our happiness.* Many times our happiness is not frustrated because life treats us unfairly but because we make choices that move us outside of God's best design for our lives.

On that foundation an important and sometimes painful question arose in the congregation: How do you experience joy and happiness when you're going through one of life's desert places? It's the kind of dilemma that was given voice by the prophet Habakkuk. His book is the eighth of the twelve Minor Prophets at the end of the Old Testament. Habakkuk was active in his ministry sometime during the seventh century BC, which means that Habakkuk's prophecy is set against the backdrop of the decline and fall of the Judean kingdom.

Have you ever finished reading a daily news summary of all the violence and injustice in the world and, in frustration, thought, *Why isn't God doing something?* If you have, then you already understand something basic about the book of Habakkuk. The prophet's name means to "embrace" or to "wrestle." As is usually the case, the prophet's name has something to do with the message of the book. The first verses of chapter 1 set out the scope of Habakkuk's situation. He says, "How long, LORD, must I call for help, but you do not listen?" (v. 2). Have you ever wanted to say that to God? Habakkuk also says to God, "Why do you tolerate wrongdoing?" (v. 3). Haven't you wondered about that? "The law is paralyzed," Habakkuk cries, "and justice never prevails. The wicked hem in the righteous, so that justice is perverted" (v. 4). Habakkuk's prophecy is different from the prophecies of many of the other prophets. He did not speak *for* God

Joy is what comes when no matter what happens, we know we belong to God.

to the people, as many other prophets did, but rather he spoke *to* God *about* the people and the nation.

This is a powerful and emotional dialogue between Habakkuk and God. It is almost like a lovers' quarrel that threatens to destroy the relationship, were it not for a covenant of love. This dialogue comes at the end of a great period in Judah, including the reign of Josiah. Under Josiah's thirty-one-year reign, there was a spiritual revival. The religion that had been nearly lost in the years since King Hezekiah ruled was put right again. However, when Josiah died, his son became king and, like so many before him, "did evil in the eyes of the LORD" (2 Kings 23:32). The nation spiraled downward again until eventually it was overrun by the Babylonians and taken into exile. What we hear in this text is Habakkuk crying out to God during all this. He thinks that in light of what has happened, God should have already come to the rescue, so he complains to God and God answers!

The Lord says something that seems very hopeful in Habakkuk 1: "Look at the nations and watch—and be utterly amazed. For I am going to do something in your days that you would not believe, even if you were told" (v. 5). However, in chapter 2 Habakkuk complains again and God answers again. This goes back and forth until we come to chapter 3 and hear the prayer at the conclusion of this dialogue. In essence,

Habakkuk prays, "Lord, I don't see that you are doing anything good. It looks to me as if everything is going wrong and there's no sign of it being different" (v. 17, author's paraphrase).

"Yet," Habakkuk prays, "I will rejoice in the LORD, I will be joyful in God my Savior" (v. 18). Where did that come from? How do you choose joy or happiness when everything seems desolate and lost? Is there joy in the desert?

Clearly, life in this world involves some occasional desert journeys. Perhaps you have been there. If you haven't experienced it, you probably will before life is over. The pertinent question has to do with what enabled the prophet to say amid this desert experience, "Yet I will rejoice in the LORD." This is not about how to be happy when the car dies or the computer crashes or even when the retirement account gets cut in half. The struggle of Habakkuk, and the struggle that many of us know, is much deeper than that. It's when life becomes crushing. It's when you've become so disoriented that you've begun to lose hope. When you don't know how you are going to survive another day, how in the world can you say with a straight face, "Yet I will rejoice in the LORD"?

Did something change to enable Habakkuk to say at the end of this book, "I will be joyful in God my Savior"? Well, not really. In fact, things are about to get much worse. So, what is it? I can tell you what it is not. Habakkuk did not receive a nice, neat response to his dilemma. In Habakkuk's mind, if God really wanted to help, God would come down and straighten things out; God would make the government work right and make the people fall into line. Instead, God reveals to Habakkuk that God is going to allow a "ruthless and impetuous people" to swoop down on Judah and become a tool of judgment (1:6). This is not good news, but rather than become angry and depressed about it, Habakkuk chooses another way. He says to God, "I will wait patiently for the day of calamity to come on the nation invading us" (3:16). In other words, "God, I will accept that you are working on a much larger scale here than what I can see. So I'll stop trying to tell you how to be God, and I will rest. I will trust in who you are and in what you are doing."

This is always the decision we must make when life turns sour. We have the power to choose in that moment. Will we choose to accuse God and become angry with God? Or will we choose to rest in God's grace even when we can't see the end of this and, in that rest, to embrace the joy of the Lord? You see, joy is not what comes when life is to our liking. Joy is what comes when no matter what happens, we know we belong to God.

I like the way musician Steven Curtis Chapman expressed it. He said, "I have learned that while we can't always control what happens to us, we can control where we allow difficult things to fall. They either fall between us and God, and we become angry. Or we allow these things to fall outside of us and press us in closer to God."[13] There is an important distinction here. The trouble that the people in Habakkuk's time were experiencing was not just the randomness of life or the unfortunate results of living in a fallen world. Their trouble was the direct result of disobedience. This is a hard word, but one that needs to be considered. Sometimes the bad things that happen in our lives and the desert places we experience are no fault of our own; they are just part of life. But sometimes the trouble we experience is due to our own choices. And sometimes we are not very honest about that. The important question is, What will we do when the bottom falls out and life gets ugly? What will we do when the skies grow dark and threatening and nothing looks familiar anymore?

I believe what Habakkuk models for us is the truth that joy is always an option, even in desert experiences. We sometimes express this with the saying "Every cloud has a silver lining." That can mean more than a positive attitude; it can refer to a grace-enabled choice. The truth is that even in life's desert times, joyful hope is there waiting to be embraced, just as Habakkuk embraced it. There is joy even in the desert because God is there with us. That's what the book of Habakkuk is about. The prophet never really receives great answers. All Habakkuk really knows to do is to cry out for mercy based on whom he has known God to be.

That's the real issue, isn't it? Are we willing to walk by faith and not by sight? Are we willing to trust God and to choose joy in trusting God even when we cannot see how things are going to turn out? Can we live with that? Can we join Habakkuk in this grace-enabled faith that chooses to believe that God is working for God's purposes in the world and that God will bring everything (and I mean everything) in our lives to a good and blessed conclusion?

The ability to see this is the secret of true happiness. It's what Dietrich Bonhoeffer discovered while languishing in a Nazi prison, knowing he was about to be executed. In that awful desert Bonhoeffer wrote, "By good powers wonderfully hidden, we await cheerfully, come what may."[14] There is such a wonderful freedom available to us when we can learn to trust God like that. Our Lord Jesus modeled this way of living. The Bible speaks of Jesus, who "for the joy set before him . . . endured the cross" (Heb. 12:2). Do you see it? The ability to choose joy even in the desert!

Do you feel that you are in a spiritual desert right now? It's never an easy place to be, but there is a way to know the gift of joy even in the desert. It is by shifting your focus from *what* is happening to *who* is there with you. It is by shifting your energy from trying to fix it to allowing God to shape you through it. That's really what Habakkuk is talking about, and it is why he can conclude this difficult episode in his life by saying, "Though the fig tree does not bud and there are no grapes on the vines, . . . yet I will rejoice in the LORD, I will be joyful in God my Savior" (Hab. 3:17-18).

Do you hear it? This is not simply about feelings or circumstances. There is a decision being made. It is a decision made because of this sure truth: "The Sovereign LORD is my strength" (v. 19).

For Reflection

- The author asserts that "many times our happiness is not frustrated because life treats us unfairly but because we make choices that move us outside of God's best design for our lives." What do you think of this claim? How does it make you feel?

- Habakkuk expressed his faith in God even though he could not see any evidence that his circumstances would change. What resources can help us develop this kind of faith?

- How can we distinguish between problems that are simply part of life and problems that are due to our own failures or sin?

- Ultimately, Habakkuk chose joy because he was willing to "live by faith, not by sight" (2 Cor. 5:7). What are you learning about walking by faith that helps you to experience joy even in desert times?

Closing Prayer

O God, whose blessed Son came into the world that he might destroy the works of the devil and make us children of God and heirs of eternal life: Grant that, having this hope, we may purify ourselves as he is pure; that, when he comes again with power and great glory, we may be made like him in his eternal and glorious kingdom; where he lives and reigns with you and the Holy Spirit, one God, for ever and ever. Amen.[15]

5

Physical Joy

Do not grieve, for the joy of the LORD is your strength.
—Nehemiah 8:10

OUR JOURNEY TOWARD JOY brings us now to the story of Nehemiah, one of the great stories of the Bible. In this narrative, we will see joy on an entirely different plane from what we've considered so far. Although the focal point is drawn from Nehemiah 8:10, you may want to read all of Nehemiah 8. It is in a worship gathering that the people of God respond to the reading of the book of the law and to words of explanation from the priests. The writer says that the people were "weeping as they listened to the words of the Law" (v. 9). That's when Nehemiah says to the people, "Do not grieve, for the joy of the LORD is your strength" (v. 10). Did you catch it? "The joy of the LORD is your *strength*."

What does that mean? Strength is a particular part of life. When Jesus gave us the greatest command of all, what did he say? "Love the Lord your God with all your heart . . . soul . . . mind . . . *strength*" (Mark 12:30, emphasis added). Jesus was affirming Israel's confession of faith, the Shema, from Deuteronomy 6. We tend to think of "heart" as the will, the inner sense of identity. "Mind" is usually understood as the intellectual or rational capacity. "Soul" is the word we typically choose to speak of the emotional or spiritual self. What is "strength"? Right, the body or physical capacity.

This wonderful episode from the powerful and transformative ministry of Nehemiah can illustrate for us a principle that Christians should understand: the joy of the Lord has a profound physical connection. By the time we come to Nehemiah 8, the project of re-building the wall of Jerusalem is complete. That's what the book of Nehemiah is about, and it's a wonder-ful story. God put it in the heart of Nehemiah to lead the people of Israel in recapturing their vision as the people of God and in returning from exile to reinhabit the promised land. The rebuilding of the walls of Jeru-salem became the focal point of national restoration, and Nehemiah led the charge. It was not easy. Major obstacles and challenges to the project are disclosed in the early chapters of the book. However, after only fifty-two days of work, the wall was restored. The sur-rounding nations and those opposing the work were shaken when they saw how quickly the project was completed. They had to admit that only with the help of God could such a thing be accomplished.

As we come, then, to Nehemiah 8, we might ex-pect to find Nehemiah and the people breathing a sigh of relief. But that's not what happens. Instead, the peo-ple begin to realize that the completion of the wall was not the completion of the vision. Perhaps it only signaled the beginning of the vision. Maybe it was just the inauguration of the real work, which was the rebuilding of the people of God. And do you know where the people learn this? It is in worship. That's the setting of this chapter. The people are gathered in one place to open their hearts to the word of the Lord.

After building a large wooden platform in the square and making all the necessary preparations, on the appointed day, the people gathered—men, women, children, all who could understand. The author says they gathered "as one" (v. 1). Ezra took the book of the law and climbed up on the great platform before all the people. The crowd, once buzzing with excitement and anticipation, grew still and quiet. Ezra opened the book, and the people stood up. Ezra began reading the book of the law. He read, and he read, and he read some more—for six hours! And the people listened. How's that for a serious church service? Do you know what happened? As Ezra read the law and read of God's plan for his people, as they heard the story in worship, the people began to weep. They grieved over their sin. So Ezra, Nehemiah, and the Levites who were teaching the people began to help them see how they could move from mourning to renewal. They wanted the people to break out of their time of mourning and weeping and spend the day in celebration, eating, drinking, and serving others.

Now here's where we get the connection to joy. After worship, Nehemiah told the people, "Go and enjoy choice food and sweet drinks" (v. 10). We know about this, don't we? We understand something about the connection between church life and food. One of our main concerns after we have gathered for worship is how we are going to continue enacting the fellowship of the Lord's Table at shared tables of fellowship, with special feasts prepared for resurrection-day renewal. Yes, eating can be sacred and not simply consumptive and self-centered.

There is a deep connection between joy and our physical bodies. We often associate joy with eating together. After we gather with family and friends to witness the vows of a wedding ceremony, we then usually take time to celebrate the occasion with feasting and camaraderie. Birthday parties often gather around food as we celebrate the life of a loved one. Even funerals are marked by people offering their love to the bereaved by bringing food and sharing stories around tables of sacred fellowship. There's a reason for this. It's something people have always understood. As Mike Mason puts it, "Real joy is felt in the body; it can even be tasted on the tongue."[16] Joy is physical, but it's not just about food. Joy is an internal, spiritual reality that should bring a brightness to our eyes, a lightness to our step, and a smile across our face. Joy is physical!

Some of the most joy-filled memories ... are inexorably linked to physical events.

One of my favorite films is a 1987 foreign language piece called *Babette's Feast*. It's the story of two sisters, the daughters of a Danish minister. The sisters forgo love in their youth for the sake of religious piety. On entering middle age, they hire a French refugee named Babette, whose restaurant was the toast of Paris before she began associating with revolutionaries. Babette wins 10,000 francs in a lottery, and she proceeds to spend the entire sum putting on a sumptuous banquet for the residents of this remote Danish village.

The preparation, cooking, and eating take up most of the nearly two hours of the film, as a village of austere folks are warmed by this act of love and transformed during the feast into a community of joy-filled people. It strikes me as such a vivid contrast to the way we tend to approach food in American society. Our lust for fast food has harmed our lives and the earth itself in many ways. For instance, we have become utterly disconnected from the sources of our food. Children (and sometimes older persons) are amazed to discover that the milk or eggs in the refrigerator are from farm animals. We rarely experience the meaningfulness of nurturing plants that bear fruit, harvesting this fruit with our own hands, carrying this produce to the table, and then offering thanks to God for this gift of life. These things take time, but we rarely linger over a feast anymore, not in eating or, even less, in preparing. It is to our peril.

Some of the very best and most meaningful conversations of my life happened around a table of fellowship as we lingered over the last cup of coffee. Some of the most joy-filled memories that are stored in my brain are inexorably linked to physical events. This is partly what the gift of sex is about. As those made in God's image, we are not only to propagate the race but also to recognize that the joyful physical intimacy of a husband and wife is expressed in a way that reflects God's glory and self-giving love. This is why sexual intimacy outside the covenant of marriage is sinful, because it tends to serve self-centered desires more than the larger purpose of love. Too often, Christians have tried to separate the spiritual from the physical. This is a heresy as old as the church. Christianity is an incarnational, embodied way of imaging the love of God for all of creation in our fellowship with one another and our communion with the beautiful gift of God's good creation. And we especially remember that God revealed Godself to us in human flesh, the person of our Lord Jesus Christ.

Our faith is intensely physical. We eat the bread, and we drink the cup. We grab new Christians by the shoulders and throw them down under the baptismal waters. We press the oil of anointing onto the foreheads of the sick. We sing and clap and lift our hands. We shake hands and give hugs to one another when we gather as the church. It's this profound connection between joy and the physical that I think Nehemiah understood, which explains why he told the people to "go and enjoy choice food and sweet drinks" after they had been so powerfully moved in worship. We were meant to party! And if you think this is just a lighthearted and superficial element of our faith, you are gravely mistaken.

It seems to me that we are experiencing a troubling resurgence of gnosticism. It expresses itself in several ways. It is seen in a careless disregard for the body, as if one's body or the bodies of others are inconsequential. It shows up when we put all our faith in the head and begin to think that being a Christian is mostly a matter of right knowledge or right doctrine. It is evident when we devalue the world of matter, the physical world, and neglect the care of God's good creation. It is by doing and thinking these things and others like them that we produce a generation of Christians who seem to believe that the actions of the body have no connection to the vitality of the spirit. It's a dangerous way to live. Spirit, mind, and body are one. Joy is physical.

Now there's another important physical element of joy in Nehemiah 8, and it has to do with serving others.

Did you notice that as Nehemiah sent the people out to feast, he was not just sending them off to a private party? Look again at verse 10: "Go and enjoy choice food and sweet drinks, and *send some to those who have nothing prepared*" (emphasis added). Would you like to increase your own joy? Do something that will bring joy to someone else. I promise that joy will spill over on you! There is also an important connection here to one of the most essential and yet oft-neglected movements of Christian worship. From the earliest days, Jesus's followers understood that sending people from Christian worship should also include carrying the consecrated gifts of the Lord's Table to those who were unable to gather that day. This embodied movement of the community of faith, bringing the sustaining gifts of bread and wine to share grace with those who are physically hindered from joining the gathered community, is an acting out of God's initiating movements toward us in love.

So, what can you do to increase your joy? Well, let me suggest a few physical things:

1. What would it be like to reenvision some of your mealtimes so that they are no longer tasks to be accomplished but opportunities for celebrating God's good gifts?

2. Is there an appropriate rhythm of work and rest in your life? Are you observing the gift of

sabbath keeping? A legalistic approach is not in mind, but a serious and joyful reception of God's invitation to stop or cease from productivity and enjoy God's gifts of one another and of God's faithful provision.

3. Is there a level of joy that could be renewed by dusting off a game or an outdoor activity that you used to enjoy?

4. When is the last time you lingered over a cup of coffee with a friend without worrying about what had to be accomplished next?

5. Husbands and wives, what has happened to the physical intimacy of your marriage? What would it take to begin nurturing the spiritual and emotional intimacies of your marriage again so that physical intimacy can truly become a gift of God to you and a joyful celebration of your union? And I must ask right there, in the context of our sexually promiscuous world, have you lost the joy of the Lord because you are seeking sexual gratification outside the covenant of marriage?

6. Finally, how could you bring joy to others by serving them and doing something for them that would also bring joy to your heart?

These are simply examples, but I hope you get the idea. Jesus said, "Love the Lord your God with all your heart . . . all your soul . . . all your mind and

. . . all your strength" (Mark 12:30). Too many of us may have invited Jesus into our hearts, but not into our "strength," the embodied, physical reality of life as we know it. When we shift our focus from self to God and others, our perspective on life, our attitude, and even our feelings about life really do change.

So *do* something. Speak, sing, hug, write a letter, cook a meal, send a check, go for a walk, bake some cookies—*do* something to express the joy of the Lord. "For the joy of the LORD is your strength" (Neh. 8:10)!

For Reflection

- Think about how feasting is connected to worship and Christian fellowship. Why is food so often a part of our gatherings?

- Think about the connection of the physical to the experience of joy. Besides those mentioned in this chapter, what are some other physical experiences that might be part of renewing joy in our lives, both individually and together?

- How might the embodied movement of serving others spark a renewal of joy in your community of faith?

Closing Prayer

O God, the protector of all who trust in you, without whom nothing is strong, nothing is holy: Increase and multiply upon us your mercy; that, with you as our ruler and guide, we may so pass through things temporal, that we lose not the things eternal; through Jesus Christ our Lord, who lives and reigns with you and the Holy Spirit, one God, for ever and ever. Amen.[17]

6

Future Joy Now

I consider that our present sufferings are not worth comparing with the glory that will be revealed in us.
—Romans 8:18

AS A PASTOR, I engaged in countless conversations with people about their sense of well-being. Those conversations would usually gravitate to ideas about happiness and joy. Sometimes followers of Jesus want to downplay any desire for happiness, thinking that somehow "happiness" is a temporal desire and "joy" is a spiritual desire. As observed earlier, the Bible doesn't make such sharp distinctions between happiness and joy, although the contextual framing of these ideas may offer some important distinctions. It does seem that some Christians have adopted the belief that we should not expect happiness in this life but wait for eternal life. But is the promise of the gospel only for life after death?

There is certainly a ring of truth in what the apostle Paul is saying in Romans 8, isn't there? Let's look again at the context of verse 18:

I consider that our present sufferings are not worth comparing with the glory that will be revealed in us. For the creation waits in eager expectation for the children of God to be revealed. . . .

We know that the whole creation has been *groaning* as in the pains of childbirth right up to the present time. Not only so, but we ourselves,

who have the firstfruits of the Spirit, *groan inwardly* as we wait eagerly for our adoption to sonship,
the redemption of our bodies. (Vv. 18-19, 22-23,
emphasis added)

We can identify with this inward groaning, because as Christians we know that our lives have been
redeemed and we have a hope that goes far beyond
what we can see now. As we lean into this hope, however, we experience the reality of life in a world that
groans. Is Paul saying that the best we can do in this
life is to just survive until Jesus returns and everything
is set right again? Many Christians seem to have this
idea, which was reinforced by much "escapist" teaching over the years. Popular among some preachers
was a "sinking ship" idea—namely, that this world is
hopelessly broken and is "going down" to destruction.
Therefore, the best we can do is to hold on and help
others "get off" the sinking ship by coming to faith in
Jesus. But are these ideas true to biblical faith?

Could it be that this "sinking ship" mentality has
something to do with why so many Christians have
lost sight of joy? If the meaning of life in this world
gets reduced to just waiting to get rescued from it,
then happiness and joy here and now may indeed be
overrated. What if there is a different way, however, to
understand how the truth of eternity can make a difference in our lives here and now? Perhaps this is pre-

cisely what Paul is trying to say in this important text. To hear this important passage in a fresh way, here is a story that may help open the meaning.

In Mexico City, a man named Pota-lamo was selling onions. A tourist asked the price of one string of onions. After Pota-lamo told him, the tourist wanted to know the price of all the onions he was selling. At this, Pota-lama declared that he did not want to sell all the onions. When the tourist asked why, Pota-lama explained that enjoying the day in the marketplace was more important than selling all the onions at once. For him, seeing people, greeting friends, sitting in the sunlight, and talking to others were the things he loved— they were his life. Selling all his onions to one person would mean the day would be over, as well as the life and things he loved, and this he refused to do.[18]

How do we enter each new day? Do we approach our days with a mindset that all that matters is selling all our onions? Or do we realize that the joy is in the living? We admitted earlier that life in this world and at this time is serious and often just plain hard. We are often stressed, distracted, worried, and tired. Paul's question to the Galatians sounded quite contemporary: "What happened to all your joy?" (see Gal. 4:15, NLT). Why have we so often lost connection to how truly joyful life can be here and now? Could it have something to do with poor "eschatology"? That's a theological word that refers to how we think about the end of all things, eternity, and our final destiny. The Bible gives us plenty of content from which to understand properly where all of this is headed. And yet, it seems that our understanding of our final hope and destiny has been formed too narrowly and not in the robust vision of the risen Christ, who said, "I am making everything new" (Rev. 21:5).

I was raised in the faith by a group of Christians who seemed to have a keen sense of a future hope and destiny. They would often say things such as, "This world is not my home." Their weekly testimonies were sharply focused on the hope of heaven. We sang lots of songs that had to do with the return of our Lord Jesus. My people seemed to resonate with Paul's words in Romans 8, that the whole of creation is groaning in eager anticipation of its final redemption and that we, too, are groaning inwardly because now, having been born of the Spirit, we know that this short life is not all there is. We do indeed have a hope and a future in Christ Jesus that is as expansive as the mind-blowing thoughts of life eternal and heavenly existence, where things broken by sin are restored. Perhaps this is where the idea of "escaping" from this world began to take hold. However, we need to read carefully the entire story of God, which casts for us a beautiful vision of God's good and beautiful creation (Gen. 1–2) as it is set right, healed, restored, and inhabited by the re-deemed people of God. The redeemed—in the glori-ous power of resurrection—then live to worship and enjoy God forever in unbroken fellowship with God and one another in God's new creation (Rev. 21–22).

It is this "new creation" perspective that can trans-form how we understand and experience the "groan-ing" that is part of life in the "now and not yet" reality of the in-breaking reign of God in Christ Jesus. A "sinking ship" perspective does not signal faith in God's saving work, but a lack of faith in God's ability and purpose to make all things new. It also prevents us from living in this world as agents of new creation, participants with God in the work of living as "new community" people who bear witness to God's salvation. Could it be that our present struggle to know and experience deep joy is related to our failure to properly under-stand what "heaven" is really about? The biblical idea of heaven is not of an otherworldly dislocated, disem-bodied spiritual life that exists beyond our knowing. It is about the return of the Lord Jesus to complete the "new creation" project of restoring God's good and beautiful creation, where the tree of life (Rev. 22:2) once again flourishes and "no longer will there be any curse" (v. 3). Rejoice! This is not only the foundation for the joy we will experience someday but also the ground for a deep and true joy we can know here and

We are called to embrace life with joy, not because it's perfect, but because we know the end of all things.

now, even as we are aware of the "groaning" of waiting for our complete redemption.

It may seem incongruous to speak of joy and suffering together, but saints who have walked faithfully with the Lord know something about this connection. The passage we are considering from Romans 8 is clearly set within a discussion about suffering. Paul says, "I consider that our present sufferings are not worth comparing with the glory that will be revealed in us" (v. 18). This could sound like, "Just hold on and wait to be rescued out of this miserable world." However, look closely at what Paul is really saying here. He does not see suffering only as a painful by-product of living in a fallen world. Paul understands that there is a mystery involved in the trials and struggles of life that bring us closer to Christ. He just said in verse 17 that we are "heirs of God and co-heirs with Christ, if indeed we share in his sufferings." There are two perspectives at work here. One is that the promise of our glorious future as "new creation" people outweighs any bad thing we could ever experience here and now. And yet, there is also a way to live through the trials and temptations of this life so that we are drawn here and now into the very heart of God. Paul does not conceive of the world as a sinking ship that one day will be abandoned. He clearly says that even the very creation itself "waits in eager expectation" (v.

19) for Christ to come again and complete the work of "making all things new" (Rev. 21:5, NASB).

Now to really get the connection here we need to go all the way back to Genesis 3 and look at it through the lens of Romans 8:20: "For the creation was subjected to frustration, not by its own choice, but by the will of the one who subjected it." Who is that one? It is God. Do you remember the Genesis 3 story? In the aftermath of Adam and Eve's disobedience, along with the consequences announced for the first couple, a curse was pronounced on the earth itself. Humanity's fall from God's original design impacted the whole creation. It's why we experience so much in this world that seems antithetical to whom we believe God to be, because it is! But the whole story of God is about a loving Father who will not rest until everything that was ruined is set right. In the coming of our Lord Jesus Christ, God's work is not only to save us from our sins and give us the hope of life everlasting but also to redeem all of creation and to set everything right—a new heaven and a new earth. God has no intention of destroying this world. What God will destroy is "death and hell" (Rev. 20:14, KJV).

If this world is part of God's grand plan for redemption, then can you begin to see the implications this has for how we live our lives in this world? We are not simply biding our time until Jesus returns and takes us to heaven. We are engaged in the work of new creation, announcing to a lost and broken world by the way we live and do life together that God, in Christ Jesus, is bringing salvation and hope. We can thus enjoy this life, even in our labor, and experience the gift of happiness, because we know that the "end" of God's story (Rev. 22) has already burst into its middle through the incarnation of God in Jesus! We were made by God to delight in the creation and to delight in each other, to love life here and now as well as hope for the future.

So how are we to love life now when so much is broken and flawed? Perhaps it is a matter of embracing and keeping the perspective of Romans 8—that is, there is an ultimate and sure redemption for those who know Christ, but that ultimate redemption is just as redemptive for life "now" as it is for life "then." Theologian Paul Achtemeier puts it like this:

> The hope we have is more than simply a form of wishful thinking, more than the ability to persuade ourselves that things will surely be better in the future. The hope we have is sure because we already have a foretaste of its fulfillment.[19]

And what is that "foretaste"? It's what Paul mentions in verse 23. We have the "firstfruits of the Spirit." This is the source of our joy here and now.

My friend Judie Hooven knew something about this. As a young and vibrant wife, mother, and bank executive, she found herself facing a devastating cancer diagnosis. We were distressed as her church family, recognizing that unless God would miraculously intervene, Judie's husband and two young daughters would be without their wife and mother. And yet, we will never forget the impact when Judie, under this imminent threat, stood before us and boldly testified, "My life is not about cancer. My life is about the kingdom of God." It was spoken with peace, conviction, and joy! She showed us that there is genuine joy even in the "valley of the shadow of death" (Ps. 23:4, KJV).

This is our task and privilege as Christians. We are called to embrace life with joy, not because it's perfect, but because we know the end of all things. Jesus spoke of this as being "in the world but not of the world" (see John 17:11, 14-16), which has always been a challenge for us. If we have too much "of," we lose our identity as children of God. If we do not have enough "in," we lose touch with those we are trying to love to Jesus.

Among the most compelling examples of this is the story of Nathan, a church leader in Bangladesh.[20] Pastor Nathan was preparing to baptize a young man of a particular village who had come to faith in Christ. The folks gathered at a river for the baptism, when suddenly the chief of the village burst through the crowd, enraged at what was about to happen. The chief ran to the banks of the river, stood over the pastor and the new young Christian, and drew back his bow with a sharp arrow poised to pierce straight through the heart of the pastor. Pastor Nathan was just about to put the boy under the water when the chief shouted, "If you baptize him, I will kill you!" Put yourself in the pastor's place for a moment. What would you do?

Pastor Nathan breathed a prayer, looked toward heaven, and plunged that new Christian under the water, baptizing him into the household of God. The village chief slowly lowered his bow and arrow. Eventually, the village chief also came to faith in Christ and became a leader in the church in Bangladesh. During a service sometime later, Pastor Nathan had the opportunity to wash the feet of that once enraged village chief, now his Christian brother.

It seems to me that there is only one way that pastor could face such an experience and emerge with such a victory. It's because he never wavered from knowing his true destiny. He was fully prepared for the real possibility that the old chief would let that arrow fly, sending him into eternity right there in that river. Perhaps he really believed what Paul says in Philippians: "For to me, to live is Christ and to die is gain" (1:21). When we live in this world with this kind of security and assurance, rooted in the confidence of the one who is making all things new, then life is full of joy! Mike Mason says it like this, "Joy knows it's on the winning side. That's why it can rejoice even in the midst of suffering. If any of life's horrors were permanent or unconquerable, joy would be impossible."[21] But it's not impossible, because we know that no matter what happens and no matter what kind of suffering we may endure here, we are a part of the grand plan of God to restore all things. The key to experiencing joy here and now is to have a sharp focus on our true destiny. As Paul says to the Corinthians, "For our light and momentary troubles are achieving for us an eternal glory that far outweighs them all" (2 Cor. 4:17). It is this perspective that gave Paul the capacity to say, "Rejoice in the Lord always. I will say it again: Rejoice!" (Phil. 4:4).

For Reflection

- What do you think about the author's claim that a "sinking ship" idea of the world and eternity may have robbed us of joy here and now? Do you recognize this "sinking ship" idea in your view of salvation?

- In what ways might we see ourselves in the Po-ta-lamo story? How might our goals for life or even for each day affect our experience of joy?

- The author writes, "We are not simply biding our time until Jesus returns and takes us to heaven. We are engaged in the work of new creation." What are some examples of this "new creation" work in which we can be engaged in our community?

Closing Prayer

O God, your never-failing providence sets in order all things both in heaven and earth: Put away from us, we entreat you, all hurtful things, and give us those things which are profitable for us; through Jesus Christ our Lord, who lives and reigns with you and the Holy Spirit, one God, for ever and ever. Amen.[22]

Benediction

THIS BRIEF BOOK on the grace of Christian joy is offered with the prayer and sincere hope that it might inspire some of God's people to recover a deep awareness of this gift of joy, which seems so in need of renewal these days. This comes from the heart of a pastor who desires deeply that the community of faith will be formed less by an anxious and angry world and more by the happy truth of the in-breaking reign of God in Christ Jesus. So, to this end, I invite you to receive this simple word of blessing:

May you go forth in the power of the Holy Spirit
> *to live in this world as a joyful sign of the new creation.*

May your happiness derive from your secure identity
> *as a redeemed child of God*

and not from the fleeting enticements of this world.

May you be an influential voice,
> *helping God's people to remember who we are.*

And as you go into this world with joy,
> *may the grace and peace of our Lord Jesus Christ be with you.* Amen.

Notes

1. Mike Mason, *Champagne for the Soul: Celebrating God's Gift of Joy* (Colorado Springs: Waterbrook Press, 2003), 3.

2. Ted Olsen, "Martin Burnham Went Out Serving with Gladness," June 1, 2002, *Christianity Today*, https://www.christianitytoday.com/ct/2002/juneweb-only/6-10-11.0.html.

3. Mason, *Champagne for the Soul*, 24 (emphasis added).

4. Oswald Chambers, *Studies in the Sermon on the Mount* (London: Simpkin Marshall, 1941), 67.

5. Walter Brueggemann, "Psalm 100," *Interpretation* 39 (1985): 67.

6. Joni Eareckson Tada, "Joy Hard Won," *Decision*, March 2000, 12.

7. "Proper 17," The Season after Pentecost, in *The Book of Common Prayer* (New York: Seabury Press, 1979), 233, hereafter cited as BCP.

8. Kim Hall, interviewed in *The Door*, September/October 1992, quoted in "Classic and Contemporary Excerpts from August 16, 1993," *Christianity Today*, https://www.christianitytoday.com/ct/1993/august-16/reflections.html.

9. Thomas Aquinas, quoted in "The Wisdom of the Saints," *Christianity Today*, October 21, 1988, https://www.christianitytoday.com/ct/1988/october-21/reflections.html.

10. "Proper 20," The Season after Pentecost, in BCP, 234.

11. Jill Lieber, "Teen Surfer Riding Wave of Amazing Grace," *USA Today*, March 19, 2004.

12. "Proper 26," The Season after Pentecost, in BCP, 235.

13. Lindy Warren, "Steven Curtis Chapman's Silent Nights," *Christian Reader*, March/April 2002, 59.

14. Elizabeth Achtemeier, *Nahum–Malachi*, Interpretation (Louisville, KY: John Knox Press, 1986), 60.

15. "Proper 27," The Season after Pentecost, in BCP, 236.

16. Mason, *Champagne for the Soul*, 33.

17. "Proper 12," The Season after Pentecost, in BCP, 231.

18. Mark Moody, "In Search of Renewal," *Strategic Adult Ministry Journal*, no. 139.

19. Paul J. Achtemeier, *Romans*, Interpretation (Louisville, KY: John Knox Press, 1985), 143.

20. Dr. J. K. Warrick shared this story while pastoring Olathe, Kansas, College Church of the Nazarene.

21. Mason, *Champagne for the Soul*, 42.
22. "Proper 4," The Season after Pentecost, in BCP, 229.